IMMORTAL LIGHT

"AMRITA JYOTI"

Advice To Householders

MATA AMRITANANDAMAYI

Translation by
M. Neelakantan Namboodiri

MATA AMRITANANDAMAYI CENTER
San Ramon, California

IMMORTAL LIGHT
"Amrita Jyoti"
Advice To Householders

PUBLISHED BY:
Mata Amritanandamayi Center
P.O. Box 613
San Ramon, CA 94583-0613
Tel: 510-537-9417

Copyright © 1994 by Mata Amritanandamayi Center
All rights reserved
Printed in the United States of America

No part of this publication may be stored in a retrieval system, transmitted, reproduced, transcribed or translated into any language in any form by any publisher.

5 6 7 8   12 11 10 09

ALSO AVAILABLE FROM:
Mata Amritanandamayi Mission Trust
Amritapuri P.O.
Kollam Dt., Kerala 690525 INDIA

ISBN 1-879410-62-1

Contents

Preface 4
Spiritual Life 12
Archana 27
Japa 35
Temples 39
Guru 47
Service 51
Karmayoga 55
Satsang 59
Home 61
Simple Life Style 69
Food 72
Married Life 82
Training Of Children 88
Vanaprastha 94
Miscellaneous 96
Glossary 102

Preface

There is an everlasting Truth that stays immutable as time passes. To realize it is the goal of human life! From time to time, *mahatmas* (great souls), appear in our midst in human form to take our hands and guide us to that Truth. They take the message of the scriptures, and adding sweetness from their own experience, impart it to us in a style that suits our culture and time.

Mother's words show modern man, drowning in the ocean of *samsara* (cycle of birth, death and rebirth), how to taste the nectar of Eternal Bliss. They are the unfailing lights that guide all who are groping in the darkness of materialistic illusion back to the abode of the Self within.

Look at our lives. We have not only forgotten the supreme goal of life, but also lost the outer conditions required for gaining true knowledge. To awaken today's society, a society bereft of spirituality, it is essential to recast the codes of family life using practical means and to set down the rules that will guide us to the realization of the Supreme Truth.

Someone who arranges his life according to Mother's advice will not have to wander far looking for happiness. Happiness will come looking for him. With loving wisdom, She has given Her children the simple rules for a life that blends spiritual *sadhana*, service to others and surrender to God.

We can keep this lamp that She lights in the inner sanctum of our hearts shining brightly only by daily adding the oil of spiritual practice! Let us pray to Mother to help us do our small part in bringing light to this age which is engulfed in darkness.

To My Children...

Children,

These bodies of ours are not eternal. They can perish at any moment. We are born as human beings after countless other births. If we waste this life living like animals, we will have to be born again as animals before attaining another human birth.

Today there are only desires in us. There is no use working hard to fulfill them. In the end, when we are unable to achieve them, we'll waste our time grieving and lose our health. Peace of mind is what we need. That is the greatest wealth.

Children, do not think that peace of mind can be gained from worldly wealth. Don't people build air-conditioned houses and commit suicide in them? In the Western countries, there is great material wealth and all kinds of physical comforts. Yet even then people don't have a moment's peace. Happiness and sorrow depend on our minds, not on external things. Heaven and hell are here on this earth. If we understand the role and the utility of each material thing in our lives and live accordingly, we will have no cause for grief. The knowledge that teaches us how to live on this earth, how to lead contented lives in the face of obstacles, is spiritual knowledge, the mind's knowledge. That is what we should acquire first. Knowing the good and the bad sides of everything in our lives, we will have to choose the path that gives us everlasting joy. Only by striving for Self-Realization can we enjoy everlasting bliss.

Do not think that our parents or children or relatives will be with us forever. At most they will be with us only until the moment of death. Yet realize our lives don't end just by our spending sixty or eighty years here. We have many more lives still to be lived. Just as we save money in a bank for life's material needs, we should accumulate eternal wealth while we are physically and mentally fit. This we can do by chanting God's name and performing righteous actions.

We may do a hundred things right, but for one wrong act people disown us. Yet even after a hundred wrongs, God accepts us for one right action. Therefore, children, be bound only to God. Dedicate all to Him. Once children are grown up, married and able to be independent, parents should lead their lives thinking of God and engaged in devout activities. When possible, the parents may spend the rest of their lives in an *ashram*. If we continue to worry about our children, neither we nor the children benefit. On the other hand, if we spend our days remembering God and chanting His name, then our families up to seven succeeding generations will benefit from it.

Children, we should pray to God in total surrender, and live knowing Him. If we take refuge in God, we will attain Him and everything we need. We will not be lacking in anything. If we befriend the storekeeper at the palace kitchen, we may get a pumpkin. If we please the king instead, all the wealth in the treasury will be ours. If we get milk, we can have yogurt, buttermilk and butter as well. Likewise, if we take refuge in God, He will meet both our spiritual and material needs. Devotion to God will bring prosperity to us, to our families and to society.

Children, life should have order and discipline. Only then will we enjoy the bliss within us without depending on external things. Think how much we toil to pass a test or to get a job! Yet, for everlasting bliss, we have not tried until now to know ourselves. At least our remaining time should be spent for that purpose. Children, chant your mantra constantly. Do *sadhana* (spiritual practice) daily in solitude at a fixed time. Go to an *ashram* occasionally and spend some time there in silent japa and meditation. Do as much selfless service for the good of the world as time and circumstances permit.

This world has its existence in love. If we lose our rhythm, nature will lose its rhythm. The atmosphere will be poisoned. It will not be conducive for seeds to sprout, for trees and animals to grow. Crops will fail. Diseases will multiply. Rainfall will decrease. There will be droughts. Therefore, children, love each other! Impart righteousness, love and other good qualities to nature. Do not harbor anger and jealousy toward anyone. See good in everyone. Never speak ill of others. See all others as children of the same mother and love them as sisters and brothers. Surrender all actions to God and let His will prevail in everything.

Children, if someone asks about our life-style, our reply should be: "Doesn't each of us act for his or her own peace and happiness? We see mental peace in this life-style. Why should you question our basic values? You seek happiness far and wide. See how much money you spend on luxuries, on intoxicants and on things you don't really need! Why should you feel upset if we go to our *ashram* or show interest in spiritual matters?" We should develop the strength to speak openly like that. Don't be timid. Be bold. We should lead our lives nurturing our spiritual heritage within us.

It is not necessary to have any shame about our life-style; shame brings only a sense of loss. Say openly: "We have chosen this path for our spiritual peace. But for our peace, don't we still build houses, get married and work at various jobs? We achieve peace through our path. Our aim is mental peace, not liberation or a heaven that we get after death. Do *you* feel peaceful?"

Once we get on a boat or a bus, we need not continue carrying our loads on our heads. Children, surrender everything to Him. If we lead our lives with this attitude of surrender, we will be free from sorrow. He will always guard and protect us.

Amma

Spiritual Life

Children, everyone should try to wake up before five in the morning. The ideal time for spiritual practices like meditation and chanting is *Brahma Muhurta* (the period between three and six a.m.) During this period, sattvic qualities are predominant in nature. Moreover, the mind will be clear and the body energetic. It is never a good practice to continue to sleep after sunrise. We should not think of staying in bed once we are awake; it increases laziness and dullness. Those who cannot decrease the amount of sleep quickly may do it in gradual stages. Those who do regular sadhana do not need much sleep.

When we wake up in the morning, we

should rise up on our right side. Imagine that the beloved deity or guru is standing in front of us and bow down at his feet. Then we can meditate at least for five minutes, sitting on the bed. Pray with a full heart: "Dear God, let me remember You constantly today. Let each one of my thoughts, words and deeds bring me closer to You! Let me not hurt anyone in thought, word or deed! Be with me in every moment!"

Children, set aside at least half an hour in the morning and in the evening for spiritual practices. After the morning bath, the whole family should sit together to worship God. *Archana* may be performed by chanting the one hundred and eight or the thousand names of Devi of our chosen deity. We can also chant our mantra, meditate or sing hymns at this time.

Whatever action we are doing, we should be sure to keep the thought of God alive within. Whenever we sit or get up, we should prostrate in that place. It is good to cultivate the habit of considering our pen, books, clothes, vessels, and the tools for our job as imbued with Divine Presence and use them with care and respect.[1] This will help keep the thought of God alive throughout our body, mind and atmosphere. Observing our actions, others will also be inspired to follow this practice.

Children, when we meet, we should greet each other with words that awaken remembrance of God such as *"Om Namah Shivaya," "Hari Om," "Jai Ma,"* and so forth. Teach the children to do the same. *"Om Namah Shivaya"* really means "Salutations to the Auspicious." When we raise one hand to say "Bye bye" we are gesturing that we are going apart from each other whereas when we join our

IMMORTAL LIGHT 15

palms and bow down the head, our hearts come closer.

Make use of all free time at the office and elsewhere for chanting the mantra or reading spiritual books. Avoid indulging in unnecessary gossip and try to talk about spiritual subjects with others. Keep away from bad company at all costs.

Writing in a diary every evening before going to bed is a good habit. We can record in the diary how much time we have devoted to our sadhana. The diary should be written in a way that helps us see our mistakes and correct them. It should not be a mere document of other people's faults or our daily transactions.

Just before going to bed, we should meditate for at least five minutes while sitting on the bed, then bow down to our deity or guru. When doing so, we can imagine that we are holding tightly the feet of our chosen deity and we can pray with all our hearts: "Dear God, kindly forgive all the wrongs I have committed today, knowingly or unknowingly. Give me the strength to resist repeating these mistakes." We can imagine that we are lying with our head in the lap or at the feet of our favorite deity or our guru or we can imagine that the deity is sitting next to us. Let us glide to sleep while chanting the mantra. By doing this, we will keep the remembrance of the mantra unbroken during our sleep. Children also should acquire this habit. They should observe a regular schedule for sleeping and waking up.

Children, to observe two hours of silence daily is very beneficial. It will help our

IMMORTAL LIGHT

spiritual progress greatly if we are able to observe silence for one day in every week as well. One may ask, "Aren't there thoughts in the mind even while observing silence externally?" Consider the water in a dam. There are waves in the water, but no loss of water takes place. Similarly, when we observe silence, our energy is minimally lost, even though thoughts may go on in the mind. It is through talking that we lose more of the vital force. The life span of a dove which always coos is short while the silent tortoise lives for a long time. Chanting God's names is not an obstacle to the vow of silence. Silence is avoidance of worldly thoughts and talk.

A *sadhak* (one who does spiritual practice) will not have time to indulge in gossip. He will not feel like talking to anyone in a harsh manner. Those who always indulge in faultfinding will never achieve spiritual progress. Do not harm anyone by thoughts, words or deeds. Be compassionate towards all beings. *Ahimsa* (nonviolence) is the highest *dharma* (duty).

Children, we must cultivate reverence towards all great masters, monks and gurus. If they come to our home, we should receive them with proper respect and obeisance. We will become worthy of their blessings only through our humility, devotion and faith, not by our pomp and show and not through any traditional ritual alone.

Children, do not listen to those who malign masters and sages. Never listen to or indulge in derogatory talk about anyone. When we harbor negative thoughts about others, our minds become impure.

Set aside some time daily for reading spiritual books. This indeed is also a form of *satsang* (holy company). Have a book on your Guru's teachings or a book like the *Bhagavad Gita*, *Ramayana*, *Bhagavata*, *Bible* or *Koran* available for daily reading. Memorize at least one verse from it daily. In addition, read other spiritual books when time permits. Reading the biographies and teachings of great masters will help us to strengthen the spirit of renunciation and to understand spiritual principles easily. It is a good practice to take down notes while reading books and hearing spiritual discourses. These notes will certainly benefit us in the future.

Children, pray for the good of everyone. We should pray to God to give a good mind even to those who harm us. One cannot sleep peacefully when there is a thief in the neighborhood. Likewise, when we pray for the well-being of others, it is we who gain peace and quietude. Children, the mantra, "*Loka samasta sukhino bhavantu!*" (Let the whole world be happy !) should be chanted at least once daily.

Let our lives be firmly rooted in Truth. Abstain from lies. In this dark age of materialism (*Kali Yuga*), adherence to truth is the greatest austerity. We might have to tell lies now and then to protect somebody or to sustain dharma, but we must be careful not to speak lies for our own selfish purposes.

Our hearts are the shrine; that is where God should be installed. Our good thoughts are the flowers to worship Him. Good deeds form the worship, good words form the hymns and love forms the offering.

IMMORTAL LIGHT 21

In God's vision, no inside or outside exists. Still, in the beginning, Mother is asking all to meditate on Him in the heart, in order to achieve concentration.

Children, meditation is not just sitting with our eyes closed. We should take every action as worship. We should be able to experience His presence everywhere.

Make use of radio, TV and films discriminatively; only for programs that will enhance our knowledge and culture. Television is "*tele-visham*" ("*visham*" means "poison" in Malayalam, Amma's native language). If we are not careful, it can corrupt our culture, damage our eyes and drain away our time.

What we need is peace of mind. We can gain that only through the control of our mind.

We should forgive and forget the faults of others. Anger is the enemy of every spiritual aspirant. Anger causes loss of power through every pore of our body. In circumstances, when the mind is tempted to get angry, we should control ourselves and resolve firmly, "No." We can go to a secluded spot and chant our mantra. The mind will become quiet by itself.

Children, those who are unmarried, should conserve their vital energy by maintaining celibacy. To turn what we gain by this into *ojas* (vitality), we also need to do *sadhana*. With increase in ojas, our intelligence, memory, health and beauty will also increase. We will gain lasting mental quietude.

Progress is not possible without discipline. A nation, institution, family or individual can advance only by heeding the words of those who deserve respect and by obeying the appropriate rules and regulations. Children, obedience is not weakness. Obedience with humility leads to discipline.

A seed has to get buried in the soil for its real form as a plant to emerge. Only through modesty and humility can we grow. Pride and conceit will only destroy us. Live with the firm attitude, "I am every one's servant." Then the whole universe will bow down to us.

What meaning do our lives have if we cannot set aside at least one hour a day out of twenty-four for thinking about God? Think how many hours we spend reading the newspaper, gossiping and doing various useless acts! Children, we can definitely set aside an hour for sadhana if we really want it. That is our real wealth. If we cannot spare a whole hour at a stretch, keep apart half an hour in the morning and again in the evening.

Meditation increases our vitality and strengthens our intelligence. Our beauty is enhanced and our mental accuracy and health are improved. We gain the mental fortitude and patience to face life's problems. Meditate! Only through meditation can we find the treasure we're looking for.

Children, daily practice of yogic postures or *suryanamaskara* (salutations to the sun) is very good for health and for spiritual sadhana. Lack of proper exercise is the cause of many of today's diseases. If we can get somewhere in time on foot, always walk instead of taking a vehicle. It is a good exercise. Only if we have to go far should we depend on vehicles. Use a bicycle, whenever possible. This will save money, too.

Children, we should visit homes of the poor, orphanages and hospitals from time to time. We should take our family members along and offer assistance and look after the welfare of the inmates. A word spoken with love and concern will give them more comfort than any amount of money. That will lead to the expansion of our hearts as well.

Try to spend at least two or three days every month in an *ashram*. Just breathing the pure air there will purify and strengthen our bodies and minds. Like recharging the batteries, even after returning home we will be able to continue our meditation and japa.

---

[1]In India, it is customary to touch an object with the right hand middle and ring fingers and touch back the forehead, eyes or heart as a mark of respect.

Archana (Worship)

Family members should sit together and do *archana* in the morning after taking the bath. If it is not possible for all to be together, individual *archana* will suffice. If circumstances do not permit taking a bath, at least wash the hands and face, but do not break the daily practice of *archana*.

Some women experience more negative thoughts during their monthly periods. It is all the more necessary to chant the mantra during that time. In India, it is customary for women not to partake in worship with others in a group during their periods. They may sit apart and chant their mantra or perform the *archana* individually. Certain people believe that women should not chant the thousand names of Devi during this time, but Amma assures that women will commit no error by doing so. The Divine Mother listens only to the language of the heart, hence women may also chant the thousand names of Devi (Lalita Sahasranama).

As far as possible, no one in the home should be asleep in bed during *archana*. If we feel sleepy during the worship, we should stand up and continue. Children, do not forget that the subtle form of the beloved deity is present where the *archana* is being performed. It is not proper to get up and leave or talk about other things during the *archana*.

It is useful to place a picture of our beloved deity in front of us during the *archana*. Meditate for five minutes before starting the worship. Visualize the beloved deity clearly from head to foot and then again from foot to head. We should imagine that the deity from within the lotus of our hearts comes to sit on the special seat placed in front of us. We should imagine that we are offering flowers at the feet of our deity as we chant each mantra. Visualize in the heart a tree in full bloom and imagine picking and offering those white flowers from this tree. Whenever real flowers are not available or not sufficient, we may do *archana* with such mental flowers (*Manasa Pushpam*) of the heart. Such flowers, offered with devotion, are dearest to the Lord. The flowers of the heart are humility, devotion and an attitude of surrender.

Whatever binds us most, whatever is dearest to us, that is what we should offer the Lord. Doesn't a mother give her child whatever she thinks is the best?

Doing some *pranayama* (breathing exercises) before *archana* helps us gain concentration. Sit erect, close the right nostril, inhale through the left nostril, then exhale through the right nostril while closing the left. Now inhale through the right and exhale through the left. This makes one round *of pranayama*. This may be done three times. While inhaling, we should visualize that all good qualities are filling us. While exhaling, imagine that all evil qualities, bad thoughts and evil *vasanas* (tendencies) are leaving us in the form of darkness.

Akshata, whole-grain dehusked rice, washed and dried, mixed with a pinch of turmeric powder and one or two drops of clarified butter (*ghee*), may be used for *archana* instead of flowers. After the *archana*, this may be collected, and added to the cereal or rice for cooking.

When doing *archana* as a group, one person should chant the mantra and the others should repeat it. Mantras should be chanted slowly, clearly and with devotion.

In the beginning, everyone may not be able to repeat clearly every mantra in the *Lalita Sahasranama* (thousand names of the Divine Mother). In that case, everyone can respond to the chants with just one mantra. While chanting the *Lalita Sahasranama*, the response may be "*Om Parashaktyai Namaha*" or "*Om Sivasaktyaikya Rupinyai Namaha*".[2]

Do not get up immediately at the end of the *archana*. The beloved deity should be brought from the seat in front of us back into our hearts and reinstalled there. Seeing the form of the deity seated in the heart, meditate a little longer. If it is possible, it is good to sing two or three *kirtans* (hymns). After taking an injection, a patient is asked to rest for a few minutes to let the medicine spread throughout the body. Similarly, to obtain the full benefit of the mantras, we should keep the mind calm for a while after worship.

At the end of the *archana*, prostrate, then get up and, remaining on the same spot, turn around clockwise three times just as if circumambulating in a temple, then bow to the Lord.

The flowers used for the *archana* may

be put under a tree or somewhere in the yard or garden where they will not be trampled.

Children, if we can do *archana* of the thousand names of the Divine Mother daily with devotion, we will grow spiritually. There will never be lack of life's essentials, food and clothing, in a family that chants the *Lalita Sahasranama* with devotion.

Children, we should consider every name as the name of our beloved deity. Imagine that He is the one that appears in all the different forms. If our beloved deity is Krishna, then while chanting the names of the Divine Mother, imagine that Krishna has come before us as Devi. We should not think that since we are chanting Devi's names, Krishna might not like it. These differences exist only in our world, not in His.

---

[2] While doing archana with the 108 names of Amma, others may repeat the mantra, "Aum Amriteswaryai Namaha".

Japa (Chanting)

Children, in the present dark age of materialism, chanting the mantra (*japa*), is the easiest way for us to obtain inner purification and concentration. Japa can be done at any time, anywhere without observing any rule regarding the purity of mind and body. Japa can be done while engaged in any task.

Deciding to chant the mantra a certain number of times daily will help foster the japa habit. We should always keep a rosary (*mala*) with us for doing japa. A rosary can be made of 108, 54, 27, or 18 beads of rudraksha, tulasi, crystals, sandal, gems, etc., with one *Guru*

(main) bead. We should resolve to chant a certain number of rosaries daily. Children, we should always chant the mantra in our minds while walking, traveling or working. It is always advisable to obtain a mantra from a Self-Realized Master (*Sat-Guru*). Until then we may use one of the mantras of our beloved deity like "*Om Namah Shivaya*", "*Om Namo Bhagavate Vasudevaya*", "*Om Namo Narayanaya*", "*Hare Rama Hare Rama Rama Rama Hare Hare, Hare Krishna Hare Krishna Krishna Krishna Hare Hare*", "*Hari Om*", "*Om Parashaktyai Namaha*", "*Om Shivashaktyaikya Rupinyai Namaha*" or even the names of Christ, Allah or Buddha.

Try not to have any break in chanting the mantra even for a moment. Continue repeating the mantra while engaged in any task. Chanting in the mind may not always be possible at first, so in the beginning, practice japa by moving the lips incessantly—like a fish drinking water. If japa is maintained, no useless talk during work will be possible. The mind will always remain peaceful. Modern day diseases are mostly psychosomatic. Japa will bestow good health to both mind and body.

If chanting is not possible during a certain task, then pray before starting it: "Lord, give Your blessings so that I may do this work in a manner that pleases You!" At the end, pray again to the Lord for forgiving any mistakes we may have committed during the task consciously or otherwise.

If we lose our money while traveling, think how frantically we search for it! In the same way, if we are unable to do japa even for a brief moment, we should grieve: "Alas, Lord, I have lost so much time! " If there is such anguish, even the time we spend sleeping will not be wasted.

Children, even if we lose a million dollars, we can recover it. If we lose one second, we cannot get it back. Every moment that we are not remembering God is lost to us.

It is a good practice to write at least one page of mantra daily. Many people get better concentration by writing than by chanting. Try also to inculcate in children the habit of chanting and neatly writing the mantra. This will help to improve their handwriting, too. The book in which the mantra is written should not be thrown around; it should be carefully kept in our meditation or shrine room.

Temples

Children, temples are places where, at least for a short while, the remembrance of God is kindled in our hearts which otherwise are totally immersed in worldly transactions. But we should not stay bound to temple rituals to the very end of our lives. No harm can come to us if we are able to do japa and meditation daily in solitude—even if we don't visit any temple. Likewise, if we are not able to fix the Lord firmly in our hearts, even a lifetime of temple-going does not do us any good.

Don't go empty handed when going to a temple or to see a Spiritual Master. Offer something as a symbol of surrender, even if it be a mere flower.

There is a lot of difference between offering a garland of flowers bought from a shop and one that we make out of flowers picked from our home garden. When we plant the flowers, water them, pick the flowers, make the garland and take it to the temple, thoughts of God alone live in our minds. The Lord accepts anything offered to Him with intense Love. When we buy a garland at a store and place it on the deity it is only a ceremonial act while the other is a garland of pure devotion and an act of love.

Children, when we go to the temple, do not hurry to have a *darshan* (sight of Lord), then make some offering and return home in a hurry. We should stand there patiently in silence for some time and try to visualize the beloved deity in our hearts. If possible, we should sit down and meditate. At each step, remember to do japa. Amma doesn't say that the offerings and worships are not necessary, but of all the offerings we make, what the Lord wants most is our hearts!

Children, we are told to make an offering at the temple or at the feet of the Guru, not because the Lord or Guru is in need of wealth or anything else. Real offering is the act of surrendering the mind and the intellect. How can it be done? We cannot offer our minds as they are, but only the things to which our minds are attached. Today our minds are greatly attached to money and other worldly things. By placing such thoughts at the feet of the Lord, we are offering Him our heart. This is the principle behind giving charities.

Some believe that Lord Shiva is at Kashi alone or Lord Krishna is only in

Brindavan. Dear children, don't think that God is confined to the four walls of a temple or a place. He is omnipotent and omnipresent. He can assume any form of His choice. We should be able to behold our beloved deity in everything. Real devotion is being able to perceive our beloved form of God not only in the temple, but also in every living being and serve them accordingly. If our beloved deity is Krishna, we should be able to behold Krishna everywhere, in every temple whether it is Lord Shiva's temple or Devi's temple. Children, do not think that Shiva might be angry if we don't worship Him in a Shiva temple or that the Divine Mother will withhold Her blessings if we don't praise Her while going to a Devi temple. One and the same person is called "husband" by the wife, "father" by the son and "brother" by the sister. The person does not change even if other people address him differently. Each of us sees God in a particular form and name Him according to our innate tendencies and imagination. Don't we always use the same name for the same person? In the same way, for God too, we must have a beloved form and name. We may ask, "Will Keshava respond if we call him Madhava?" But, here we are not calling just an ordinary individual. We are addressing the omniscient Lord. He knows our mind. He knows that we are addressing Him whatever name we use.

Children, we may go to the temple, reverently circumambulate the sanctum sanctorum and put our offering in the charity box, but on our way out if we kick the beggar at the door, where is our devotion? Compassion towards the poor is our duty to God. Mother is not saying that we should give money to every beggar that sits in front of a temple, but do not despise them. Pray for them as well. When we hate others, it is our own mind that becomes impure. Equality of vision is God.

Temple festivals are meant for the spiritual and cultural awakening of the common people. Nowadays, the programs associated with temple festivals very often do not serve their purpose. In the temple premises, we should hold only those programs that nurture spirituality in us. The temple air should be vibrant with Divine Names. Once we enter the temple courtyard, we should put an end to all useless talk. Our minds should immerse themselves completely in the thought of God. Children, regaining the sanctity of temples is the responsibility of all householders. Therefore, those who are concerned about our spiritual heritage should work with temple committees to find a remedy for today's pitiable state of affairs.

Many priests and employees at temples work for pay. No one should judge religion on the basis of the shortcomings of such workers. We should frame suitable rules and regulations for preventing them from falling prey to material temptations. The true guiding spirits of religion are those who engage in selfless service while dedicating their entire lives to attaining the vision of God.

Isn't it human beings who impart vitality to the image in the temple? If no one sculpts the stone, it doesn't become an image. If no installs it in the temple, it does not acquire any sanctity. If no worship is done, it does not acquire any power. Without human effort there cannot be any temples. What is wrong then in saying that we should view great masters as equal to God? Temples installed by such spiritual masters have a special energy of their own.

In ancient times, there were no temples. There were only lineages of gurus and disciples. Temples are for weaker minds. We teach blind children using braille letters. One may ask why we do this; why not teach them just like other children? No, that is not enough. For those who cannot see, we need to do it in this special way. Likewise, people of this age need temples to connect their minds to God.

Renovating temples does not mean building great gate towers or receptacles for offerings. What we should focus on is the regular conduct of worship according to tradition, regular satsangs (spiritual discourses), devotional singing and so forth. Our devotion and faith give life to temples, not rituals and ceremonies. Children, we should remember this when we are involved in temple matters.

Guru

Ashrams and the Gurukulas are the pillars of spiritual culture. If we perform sadhana according to the guru's advice, we need not go anywhere else. We will get whatever we need from the guru.

※

Children, we can grow spiritually only if we see the guru as the manifestation of God. We should not accept anyone as guru before we are fully convinced personally that he is authentic and truthful. Once we choose someone as guru, we should surrender completely to him. Only then will spiritual development be possible. Devotion to the guru means total surrender to him.

※

With the exception of very few who have gained higher spiritual tendencies in prior lives, Self-Realization is not possible for anyone without the blessings of a guru. Think of the guru as the manifestation of God in this world. Take even the most insignificant word of the guru as an order and obey it. That is the real service to the guru. There is no greater austerity. The guru's blessings flow automatically to any obedient disciple. That is the real *guruseva* or service to the guru. There is no greater austerity. The guru's blessings flow automatically to an obedient disciple.

The guru is not someone who is confined to the body. When there is selfless love for the guru, we will be able to see him not only in his body but in every living and nonliving thing in this world. Learn to see everything as the guru's body and to serve them accordingly.

The ashram is Mother's body. Mother's soul is in Her children. Children, all the service done for the ashram, is done for Mother. The ashram is not anyone's private property. It is the means to provide peace and quietude for the entire world

---

Those children who receive a mantra from Mother should lead a disciplined and orderly way of life. They should give up bad habits such as drugs, smoking and drinking. They should observe celibacy until marriage. Even after marriage, they should follow Amma's advice in living together. Children, we should disclose everything to our guru and hold back no secret from Him. The disciple must have the same love and attachment for the guru that a child has for its mother. Then only can we have spiritual growth. Japa and meditation should be practiced daily without fail. Only by putting our mantra into regular practice can we benefit from it. Book knowledge of agriculture is not enough; we have to apply it to get good crops.

To Mother, all are Her children. In Mother's eyes no defect of Her children is serious. But when She is considered as the guru, it is essential for the growth of the disciples that they conduct themselves according to the tradition. Mother will pardon all the mistakes of Her children, but nature has certain laws. That is what brings punishment for our sins. Children, we should be able to take any sorrow or suffering as conducive for our growth.

Service

Children, we should simplify our life's needs and use the resulting savings for charity. Contribute to charitable projects like the printing and publication of spiritual books so that they can be sold at a lower price. Poor people will then be able to buy and read them. In this way we can help to cultivate spiritual culture in them also.

Remember to set apart at least one hour every day to do some service for others. While the food we eat nurtures our bodies, it is what we give in charity that nurtures our souls. If time is not available daily, reserve at least a few hours every week for some worthwhile act of charity.

It is not good to give money to all those who beg; give food or clothing instead. They may misuse the money we give for drinks and drugs. We should not give them a chance to err. Try not to see them as beggars, but as God Himself. Thank Him for giving us a chance to do His service. It is better to serve the beggars no food at all rather than serving them spoiled food on dirty plates. Never give anything with contempt. Loving words and deeds are the best alms.

It is auspicious to conduct ceremonies associated with our life such as naming, first feeding, starting education, weddings etc., in a temple or ashram and to give food and clothing to the needy on such occasions. The expenses for wedding feasts and decorations should be kept to a minimum so the savings can be utilized for some poor girl's marriage expenses or for some child's education.

Renunciation should become a part of our lives. If we're accustomed to buying ten new outfits of clothes every year, cut down the purchases by one this year. Cut down one more next year. Thus we can reduce our wardrobes to just what we really need. The money saved by ten people in this manner would be enough to build a house for some deserving person such as one who is handicapped or destitute. This in turn may encourage them to become a devotee. Many others will also improve their ways seeing our righteousness and selflessness. Cut down the luxuries, not only in clothing but also in everything else and use the money saved in this way for charitable purposes.

We must set aside a certain part of our income for helping others. If it is not possible to give the money directly to the needy, it may be given instead to ashrams or spiritual organizations engaged in service activities. We may, for example, make spiritual publications available to school, college and public libraries. Our unselfish and compassionate acts will not only help others, but will also help to broaden our minds as well. One who picks a flower for offering is the first one to enjoy its fragrance and beauty. Likewise, it is our own self that is awakened through our selfless acts. Our very breath, suffused with good thoughts, benefits others as well as Mother Nature.

Children, when you serve the world selflessly, you are serving Mother Herself.

Karmayoga

Children, however high our position in life, we should always think that we are just a servant of our fellow men. Think that God has given us this position so that we may help them fulfill their needs. Humility and modesty will then dawn in our hearts automatically. When we work with the attitude that we are serving God, work will become a sadhana. Treat everyone at the place of work, superiors and subordinates alike, with love and friendship. The way we treat others determines how the world treats us.

Children, when a superior takes us to task, consider it an opportunity provided by God to eliminate our ego and wipe off the hostile feeling that may arise in us. Similarly, when we have to deal sternly with subordinates, take care not to let hatred or irritation rise inside us. In the eyes of a true spiritual aspirant, superiors, subordinates and colleagues are all different forms of God.

We should never think that we are working for our boss or for the company. We should do our duty with the attitude that we are serving God, then our work will not be just putting in time for earning a salary. We will be sincere and attentive in our work. The first quality that a spiritual aspirant should have is complete *sraddha*[3] (awareness and attention) for the work at hand.

We should always be ready to do extra work over and above what is required by the rules. Only such additional work, done without any desire for praise or reward, will qualify as selfless service.

Placing a picture of our beloved deity or guru at our place of work in a clearly visible position will help us hold the thought of God steadily in our minds. There is no need to be ashamed of this. Our example will be a model for others.

"I am an important person; I hold a high position in society. How can I go to the temple and worship in the jostling crowd there? How will I bow down before the Lord? Isn't that demeaning?" Thoughts like these arise from the ego. Be ready, always, anywhere, to repeat the Lord's name and to pay homage to the Lord and the guru. We don't gain anything from a certificate of greatness from society; what we need is a certificate from God.

With constant effort, we will be able to repeat the mantra in our minds even while doing any type of job. Only actions accompanied by the remembrance of God is real *karma yoga*. The work that we do with the attitude that it is God's work does not cause bondage.

---

[3]*Sraddha* in Sanskrit means faith rooted in wisdom and experience whereas the same term in Malayalam is used to denote attentive awareness in any action. Amma often uses the term in the latter sense.

Satsang

Children, getting together in a temple or *ashram* for devotional singing and *satsang*, instead of wasting time gossiping or seeing movies, is beneficial for us and for the environment. Alternatively, we can sit alone in solitude and meditate or sing hymns.

Do not hesitate to invite friends and co-workers when holding *satsang*.

Make it a habit to get together once a week, at a fixed place or in different homes by turn, for *archana*, *bhajan* and meditation. If we distribute some fruits or sweets as *prasadam* (sanctified offerings), children also will become interested in attending these gatherings. The spiritual culture acquired in childhood will stay alive in their adult life too. Those who take part in these spiritual gatherings may bring along some *Akshata* (rice), and a common meal also can be served. This will bring inner purification and strengthen the sense of unity and brotherhood. The *archana* and worship will remove all harm which may arise due to the displeasure of departed ancestors or malefic planetary influences. The environment will be purified. Participation in *satsangs* will make our hearts full with thoughts of God.

Home

Give a place to God in every undertaking. Those who cannot build a separate room for worship can set aside at least part of a room for *japa*, meditation and spiritual study. That spot should be used only for spiritual practices. God should not be relegated to the space under the stairway. We should live as God's servants and not put Him in a servant's place.

At sunset a lamp filled with clarified butter or any vegetable oil should be lit and everyone in the household should gather near it to sing hymns and do a little meditation. There is no need to compel anyone to participate in worship. Do not be troubled if someone is not joining. Saying prayers at sunset was a common practice in every household in the olden days (in India). Today it is going out of fashion and we are suffering the consequences of this neglect. At dusk, the juncture of day and night, the atmosphere is impure. Through meditation and singing devotional songs, we gain one-pointedness of mind which will purify our minds and the atmosphere. Instead, if we engage in loose talk or fun, worldly vibrations will pollute our minds further.

Children, we should always strive to cultivate the vision of unity, not of diversity. There is no need to place anything other than the pictures of the beloved deities of the family members and of the guru in the meditation room. The room and the pictures should be cleaned daily. Some people will have some special pictures of gods and goddesses to be hung on festival days like Krishna's birthday, Shivaratri, etc. There is nothing wrong in doing so. Milk, by any name, is the same nourishing substance. Likewise, the Lord, even though He is known by many names, is only One. It is good to hang a picture of our guru or beloved deity in a visible place in every room. Dusting and cleaning them daily will help enhance *sraddha* (awareness and attention) and devotion.

Children, in former times in India, every house had a sacred *tulasi* (basil) plant and a spot to grow it. Also, it was a common practice to grow plants that produced fragrant flowers for daily worship. Today, their place is taken by decorative plants and cactus. These reflect the change in the inner disposition of people. A basil plant or *crataeva* tree are considered holy and believed to bring prosperity to the house where they are nurtured and revered. They should be watered daily and whenever we go out or come into the house we must offer our salutations to these plants. The ancients used to touch Mother Earth in reverence before planting their feet on the ground when they got up from the bed in the morning. They used to bow to the rising sun as the embodiment of divinity and giver of life. They lived in harmony with Nature. They saw God's essence in everything. They had joy, peace and health born of this attitude.

Plants such as *tulasi* and many fragrant flowers used for worship have medicinal qualities as well. Growing them near the house is good for purifying the atmosphere. Those who have enough land around the house may grow a little flower garden. We should always chant our mantra while gardening. At the same time, the awareness that the flowers are for worship will help to retain the remembrance of God within us.

Each household should use a portion of its land for growing trees and plants. This will purify the environment. It will maintain Nature's harmony. In the old days, each house had a grove and a pond attached to it. Not only the householders, but the whole society enjoyed their benefits.

Children, the auspiciousness of a house does not come from its external glitter but from its cleanliness. Pay daily attention to keeping the house and surroundings clean. Don't think it is the task of the women or of any one particular person. Instead, every one at home should work together on it. Traditional customs such as not entering the house wearing street shoes and keeping water outside the house for people to wash their feet before entering help foster a spiritual sense of reverence towards our abodes.

Children, treat domestic help with dignity. Do not hurt their self-respect. Do not give them leftover food. We should treat them like our own brothers and sisters.

Children, see the kitchen as a place of worship. It should be clean and orderly. Cooking should be started only after the morning bath and with the repetition of the mantra. We should behold the sweet form of our beloved Guru or deity in the flames. Imagine that we are cooking the food as an offering for Him. Visualize that He receives the essence of food before it is served on the table. Before retiring at night, the kitchen should be swept clean. All the dishes should be cleaned and set aside to drain. Take care not to leave any food uncovered.

There was a time when children in a home would express love and show respect toward their parents and elders.[4] That has, for the most part, been lost now. Householders should set a model for children by paying respect to their parents. How will the children show respect to their parents who neglect and show disrespect to their own aged parents? Parents should always set an example for their children to follow.

If you are leaving the house on some errand, go only after paying your respects to your elders. Children should make a habit of taking leave of their parents before going to school. It is humility and modesty that draw the grace of God to us.

Everyone in the family should take part in the household chores. This will help foster love among family members. Men should not treat kitchen work as meant only for women and stay away. They should help as much as possible. Also, give small children chores that they can handle.

---

[4]In India, it is customary to touch the feet of elders, parents, monks or Guru with both hands and touch back the forehead, eyes or heart to show one's respect. In earlier days this was practiced in every household by all children as the first act on getting up in the morning or leaving the house for school.

Simple Life Style

Children, build up selflessness and reduce efforts to increase personal comforts. A spiritual aspirant should not be a pleasure seeker. Try to lead a simple life, reducing personal possessions to a minimum.

Children, with a little care, we can save a good part of the money unnecessarily spent on building a house. People usually spend everything they have saved for building a house and end up in debt. One should have a reasonable house to live in. Avoid all additional luxuries. Children, when we build a house worth hundreds of thousands for a family of just four or five members, don't forget that there are countless poor, homeless people who spend their nights out in the rain and cold.

It is good to avoid clothes with bright or splashy colors. This helps us stay clear of others' attention. When others pay attention to us, our attention may wander in their direction too. We should try our best to cultivate simplicity in our clothes and lifestyle. Women should give up the craving for jewelry. Children, good words and deeds are the real jewels.

Do not throw away old clothes; clean them and give them to the needy.

Children, always act without any expectation of the fruit of the action. Expectation is the cause of all our grief. We should dedicate our lives to the Lord. Trust that He will guard us. What we should gain through family life is the training for total surrender to God. We have to realize that our wife and little ones do not belong to us or we to them. Children, have absolute faith that everything is His alone. Then He will take over all our burden; He will take our hand and lead us to the goal.

Food

Children, not a grain of the food we eat is made purely by our own effort. What comes to us in the form of food is the toil of our fellowmen, the bounty of Nature and God's compassion. Even if we have millions of dollars, we still need food to satisfy our hunger. Can we eat dollars? Therefore, never eat anything without first praying with humility.

※

Children, we should always eat our food sitting down. Do not eat standing or walking around.

※

While eating, our attention should not be focused just on the taste. Imagine that our chosen deity or Guru is present within us and that we are feeding Him. This will turn eating into a *sadhana*. Do not talk while eating. When feeding children, too, we should think that we are feeding our beloved deity. As far as possible, everyone in the family should eat together. Take a little water in your right palm and chant the *bhojana mantra*[6] or your own mantra. Then pass your hand clockwise over the food three times and sip the water. Close your eyes and pray for a couple of moments: "Dear God, let this food give me strength to do Your work and to realize You."

If we have some pet animals or birds, we should feed them also before taking our food. Perceive God in every living being and feed them with that attitude.

Food should be consumed with *mantra japa*. This will purify the food and the mind at the same time.

The mental disposition of the one who prepares the food is transmitted to all those who consume it. Therefore, as far as possible the mothers should do the cooking for the entire family. If it is done while chanting the mantra, the food will benefit everyone in a spiritual way.

Children, consider food to be the Goddess Lakshmi (the goddess of prosperity), and receive it with devotion and reverence. Food is *Brahman* (the Absolute Being). While eating, never talk about anyone's faults and shortcomings. Eat the food as the Lord's *prasadam*.

After prayers, and before eating anything, it is a good custom for everyone to feed feed one another a small portion of the food. This will help to cultivate mutual love and affection among the family members. In India, in olden times, the wife would take the leftovers from the plate of the husband, considering it as God's *prasadam*. In those days, the husband was considered by the wife as a visible form of God. Today, where can we find such a wife or a husband who deserves this? Every man would like to be treated like that by his wife, but who is ready to lead a life worthy of that reverence? Every man would like to have a wife like Sita, the chaste wife of Lord Rama, but no one bothers to think whether they live like Rama.

Children, we cannot control our mind without controlling our desire for taste. The health aspect, not the taste, should be the prime criteria in choosing the food. We cannot relish the blossoming of the heart without foregoing the taste of the tongue.

Those of us who are doing *sadhana* should take care to eat only plain, fresh, vegetarian food (*sattvic food*). It is good to avoid food that is excessively salty, sweet, hot or sour. It is the subtle essence of what we eat that becomes our mind. Purity in food helps to develop mental purity.

Children, breakfast should be light. It is better if we can do without it. Eat a desired quantity at lunch. Eat light at night.

Children, we should not fill our stomach all the way. Leave a quarter of it empty. This will help our bodies to digest the food properly. If we eat until we can't even breathe, we also increase the work load of our heart.

Overeating will harm not only our *sadhana*, but also our health. Children, we should give up the habit of eating something every now and then. Observing regularity in time and quantity in eating is good for health and mental control. Eat to live; do not live to eat.

It is a very good practice to eat only one meal on weekends and do *japa* and meditation at home or in an *ashram*. Going gradually from one meal on that day to complete fasting will improve the *sadhana* and general health. Eat only fruits if complete fasting is not possible. Full moon and new moon days are good days for fasting.

Do not eat at twilight. It is said in the ancient epics that it was during the twilight that Lord Vishnu killed the demon Hiranyakashipu. The air is most impure at that hour. It is not the time to fill the stomach. It is the time to repeat the Lord's name and fill the mind instead.

※

It is good to take laxatives twice a month to have the bowels cleared thoroughly, especially for those who do *sadhana*. Accumulation of feces inside will hinder concentration. It will pollute the thoughts.

※

Mother is not asking those who eat meat and fish to stop doing so abruptly. But it is good for *sadhana* to switch over to a completely vegetarian diet gradually. Children, it is very difficult to put an abrupt stop to any habit. Study the mind and bring it under control over time.

Everyone knows that smoking and drinking are injurious to health. Still, most people who have cultivated these habits find them hard to give up. How can someone who cannot free himself from the clutches of a cigarette aspire to attain God-Realization? Those who cannot give up smoking abruptly should try chewing a substitute like cardamom or licorice or sipping some water when the urge to smoke comes up. If we try sincerely, we can completely give up smoking or any other bad habits in a short time.

Coffee and tea may give a temporary lift, but making them a habit is in fact harmful to our health. Give them up as well.

Dear children, we should make a firm resolve to give up alcohol totally. Drinking ruins health, mental strength, wealth and the peace of the family, all at the same time. Do not drink alcohol even to please our friends.

※

Children, do not use intoxicants of any sort. We who should be serving the world should not ruin our health by smoking and drinking. The money we waste on these things can be used for so many useful things. With the money we smoke away, we can buy an artificial leg for one who has lost a leg, pay for an eye operation for someone with a cataract, or buy a wheelchair for a polio victim. Or, if nothing else, we can buy some spiritual books for the local library.

※

To let food spoil or to discard it half-eaten is a harm to society. Think of how many people suffer without even one meal a day. When a neighbor starves, can we be happy eating a sumptuous feast? We have to help the hungry as best we can. We have to see that feeding the hungry is no less than the worship of God.

---

[6]*Aum Brahmarpanam Brahma havir
Brahmagnau Brahmana hutam
Brahmaiva tena gantavyam
Brahma karma samadhinah.*

Married Life

Children, husband and wife should love and serve by seeing God in each other. They should thus be ideal couples, models for their children and for others.

***

When husband and wife together worship the Lord, do meditation and *japa*, read spiritual texts, serve the world, turn their home into an *ashram*, and thereby progress in their *sadhana* together, they need not seek liberation. It will come to them automatically.

***

The husband and wife should not hinder each other on the spiritual path. One should not give up spiritual pursuits even

IMMORTAL LIGHT 83

if it is not approved by the spouse. Yet it is also wrong to turn away from our duty in the name of spiritual practice. Mother has seen many people doing this; it is never right. When it is time to perform our tasks, we should do them with the remembrance of God. If, instead, we sit for meditation at that time, there will not be any progress. We should not be a cause of pain to the spouse who is against our *sadhana*. Instead, while performing the family duties, pray to God to bring a change in the mind of our spouse.

Couples should abstain from sexual relations at least two or three days a week. Gradually try to reach a stage of celibacy most days. Avoid sexual relations on full moon and new moon days and when the wife is going through her monthly periods. Try to gather the strength to live as brother and sister after one or two children are born. This is essential for reaping the full benefit of *sadhana* and to make spiritual progress through mental restraint.

Each time we have sex, we should ask the question: "O mind, where does this joy come from? Isn't this only draining my strength?" Any pleasure gained by means other than mental control weakens the body. The relation between the husband and wife should turn into a love of the heart untouched by desire. Make progress in the path of virtue, keeping the mind fixed solely on the Supreme Being.

Children, one baby is enough. At the most two; not more than that. With fewer children, we will be able to raise them with care. Mothers should insist on breast-feeding their children. Remember the Lord's name when feeding and pray:

"Dear God, bring this child up to serve the world! This is your child. Bestow your own qualities on him." Then, the child will be intelligent. He will be hard working and become prosperous. We only need to keep God in our thoughts for everything to turn out in our favor.

Married men should avoid relations with other women. Likewise, married women should not seek other men.

When there is a difference of opinion in the family, be ready to discuss the matter and resolve the issue the same day instead of postponing it. Anyone can return love for love—there is nothing great about that. Try to return love for hatred. This alone is the true measure of our greatness. Only when we are ready to forgive and accommodate each other's faults and shortcomings will peace prevail in the family. For moulding the children's character, it is essential that the parents lead a model life. When the parents' lives are far from exemplary, how can they bring up the children in the proper manner?

Children conceived during the twilight hours turn out to be idiots or bad tempered. Worldly thoughts are at a peak during this time. That is why it is all the more necessary to do worship, archana, japa, and meditation during twilight hours.

Anyone who practices diet control, *japa* and meditation regularly will in due course gain the strength to maintain celibacy. But during some stages of *sadhana* innate tendencies may flare up and this may cause a strong reawakening of worldly desires. Seek the Guru's advice at this point. Seek refuge in God without fear and maintain self-control as far as possible.

Couples should observe strict celibacy when the wife is 3-4 months pregnant. Avoid all discussions, movies and magazines that arouse worldly desires and passion. Instead, read spiritual books daily, do japa and meditation. The mother's thought waves and emotions play an important role in moulding the character of the child in her womb.

Practice *of pranayama* (breath control) without firm abidance in celibacy may lead to complications. Practice *of pranayama* should be done only under the supervision *of* the Guru.

Training Of Children

Up to the age of five, children should be given a lot of love. From the age of five to fifteen they should be brought up under strict discipline especially regarding their study. It is at that time that life's foundation is formed. Love without discipline will only spoil them. Above the age of fifteen children should be given maximum love otherwise they may go astray.

※

Many teenage boys and girls have told Mother that lack of love at home causes them to go astray. During their teens children yearn for love while the parents punish and scold them severely to discipline them. They don't even allow the teenaged children to come near them, let alone show the children any love. Showing excessive affection at a time when the children need to be taught discipline will spoil them, and they will become lazy and indifferent to their studies. But when they are older, they should not be reprimanded severely, instead, their mistakes should be pointed out and corrected by reason and logic.

Parents should start explaining spiritual ideas to children at an early age. Even if they acquire bad habits when they grow up, the good impressions dormant in their subconscious mind will bring them back to the right path in due course.

Do not abuse or speak ill of anyone in front of children. Children will imitate you. Wealth will come today and will be gone tomorrow but good character will last the whole life. Therefore, rich parents also should ensure that their children grow up to become humble and self-reliant.

Children should be taught to be humble towards teachers and spiritual masters. Learning, especially that of a spiritual nature, will be fruitful only in the soil of humility. There are those who think children attending school need not do any other work. That is not right. School education is not enough for life. Children should learn to do all the tasks at home.

Parents who sing lullabies and tell stories to children at bed time should use hymns and spiritual stories for this purpose. This will also help the children keep God alive in their thoughts. The spiritual culture will take deep roots in their subconscious. Be selective in choosing books for them to read as well.

Children's mental maturity will depend on the training given by grown-ups. The parents and elders at home should pay attention to matters connected with the education of children. Those who are educated should help the children with their lessons as much as possible. Don't leave the entire responsibility to the teachers. If there are children in the neighborhood going to school with your own children, you can invite them also and teach them together. That is what good neighbors should be doing. Never should one find pleasure in the failure of the child in the neighboring house and desire the success of the highest grade only for one's own.

Children should respect their elders. Rising when elders enter the room, sitting down only after they take their seat, answering them politely, obeying their instructions, refraining from making fun of them or answering them loudly or in a contrary way, these are all essential for the welfare of the family. Similarly, when little children ask for permission to go outside, grown-ups should give their permission by a loving kiss. Children should have the feeling that they are loved. Our love for children should not be like honey hidden inside a stone.

The foundation for all rituals and customs should be love. Mere acts without appropriate attitude is useless. Everything should be done with humility, devotion and a pure motive. For discipline to develop, there should be humility and obedience. Our humility and obedience are like the grease for a machine: if we run the machine without the lubrication, it will certainly be ruined.

Children should be brought up with an understanding of their culture and should take pride in it. They should be given names that reflect their culture and evoke the remembrance of God and spiritual masters. From a young age, instill good impressions of God in them by telling them stories of the Lord and saints. At one time in India, everyone used to learn Sanskrit, the language of the scriptures, from a very young age. This helped them to absorb the seeds of spirituality early in their lives. Even people who did not learn the scriptures formally were able to lead lives based on spiritual principles by being associated with those who had been taught.

Vanaprastha (Retired life)

Once the children are grown up and are able to take care of themselves, husband and wife should go to an *ashram* and lead a spiritual life, working for their spiritual improvement by engaging in meditation, *japa* and selfless service. It is necessary to cultivate from the beginning of one's spiritual life an attitude of strong attachment only to the Lord in order to make this transition possible. Without such a spiritual bond, the mind will cling to its ties; first to the children, then to the grandchildren and so on. This kind of clinging is of no use to us or our children. Our lives will be a waste if we allow our clingings to persist! If, on the other hand, we spend our lives in *sadhana*, our spiritual power will help both us and the world. Therefore, cultivate the habit of withdrawing the mind from countless worldly subjects and turn it totally towards God. When we pour oil from vessel to vessel in succession we lose some at each step; in just the same manner, by attaching the mind to many things, we lose whatever little spiritual power we have. By collecting water in a storage tank, it can reach all the faucets equally. Likewise, by keeping our mind on God constantly, while engaged in any work, the benefit will reach all members of the family. The ultimate aim in life should not be to amass wealth for children and relatives; it should be to focus on our own spiritual development.

Miscellaneous

Children, the soul is nothing but God. True austerity is action undertaken with an unbroken awareness of God.

※

Children, meditation and *japa* are not the only forms of *sadhana*. Selfless service is also *sadhana*. And it is the easiest path for self-unfolding. Even when we buy flowers for a friend, it is we who enjoy their fragrance and beauty first. In the same way, through selfless service our heart is expanded. It is we who enjoy the happiness first.

※

Before we pray for ourselves, we should pray that our neighbors be given goodness of heart and mind. If there is a robber or a madman next door, how can we sleep peacefully? We will be constantly worried about being robbed. We won't have the peace of mind to leave home for a minute. We should pray to God that our neighbors become good. This is for our own peace and quiet. Only through such prayers for others can we unfold spiritually and attain purity of heart.

Children, do not look for and talk about the faults and failures of others; always try to see only the good in everyone instead. When we injure our hand, we don't blame the hand, but apply medicine to the wound and nurse it with great attention. We should serve others with the same intensity without blaming them for their faults.

When we step on a thorn and it pierces the sole of our foot, no amount of crying will get rid of the thorn or the pain. We have to pull the thorn out and put some medicine on the wound. In the same way, there is no use crying about illusory things that give us pain. If the same tears are for God, our mind becomes clean and we gain the strength to overcome all obstacles. Therefore, dear children, surrender everything to Him and be strong! Be full of courage!

Children, crying for God is not a weakness. Those tears wash away the impurities which are the bad habits accumulated during many lives. The candle burns brighter and with more luster as it melts down. Likewise, tears for God hasten our spiritual growth. On the other hand, when we weep for worldly objects or for our family, our strength is lost and we become feeble.

Once we are in the bus, why go on carrying our load, crying about how heavy it is? We should put the load down. In the same way, surrender everything at His lotus feet. He will guard and protect us. We have sorrows today because we do not surrender.

Children, whatever act we are engaged in, be aware that it is through His power that we act. We often see road signs made with reflective paint. When light falls on the paint, it shines. In just the same way, it is only by His power that we are able to function. Know that He makes us do everything. We are only the instruments.

The concentration we need to count the grains in a handful of sand, the concentration we need to walk across a river on a tight rope, that is the concentration we should have in everything we do.

Children, *ahimsa* (the principle of non-injury) should become the vow of our lives. *Ahimsa is* refraining from causing pain to anyone through thought, word or deed.

Only through opening our heart and mind can we find His world which is full of bliss in the midst of this world which is full of hurdles. Children, without a spirit of forgiveness and humility, we cannot know God or earn the guru's grace. The man of courage is one who can forgive even when anger rises uncontrollably. When we press down the button, the umbrella unfolds and gives us protection from rain and sun. But if the button refuses to go down, nothing happens. When the seed goes under the soil, it sprouts and becomes a tree. When it is a tree, we can tie even an elephant to it. But if the seed refuses to surrender, refuses to get out of the seed basket and go underground, it may end up as food for a mouse.

Children, if you love Mother, then see Mother in every living thing and love it as such.

Children, God-Realization and Self-Realization are one and the same. God-Realization is nothing but the ability and expansiveness of heart to love everything equally.

Glossary

AHIMSA : Abstaining from killing or giving pain to any living being in thought, word or deed.

ARCHANA: A mode of worship by repetition of one hundred, three hundred or a thousand names of a deity.

ASHRAM: Hermitage or residence of a sage

BHAGAVAD GITA: The teachings of Lord Krishna to Arjuna at the beginning of the Mahabharata war. It is a practical guide for the common man for every day life and is the essence of Vedic wisdom. Bhagavad Gita literally means "The Song of God"

BHAGAVATAM: The book about the incarnations of Lord Vishnu, especially Krishna. It upholds the supremacy of devotion.

Bhajan: Devotional singing
Dharma: Righteousness, in accordance with Divine Harmony
Guru: Spiritual Master/Guide
Guruseva: Service to the spiritual Master
Japa: Repetition of a mantra
Kali Yuga: The present dark age of materialism
Karma: Action
Kirtan: Hymn
Lalita Sahasranama: Thousand names of the Universal Mother in the form of Lalitambika
Mahabharatam: Great epic written by Vyasa
Mahatma: Great soul
Mala: Rosary
Mantra: Sacred formula, the repetition of which can awaken one's spiritual energies.
Ojas: Sexual energy transmuted into spiritual energy by spiritual practices.
Prasadam: Consecrated offering distributed after worship

PRANAYAMA: Controlling the mind through breath control.

SADHAK: One dedicated to attaining the spiritual goal, one who practices sadhana (spiritual discipline)

SADHANA: Spiritual practices

SAMSARA: The cycle of birth, death and rebirth

SAMSKARAS: Mental tendencies accumulated from past actions.

SANNYASIN: A monk or renunciate

SATSANG: Company of the wise and virtuous; also a spiritual discourse by a sage or scholar

SATTVIC: The quality of purity or serenity

SRADDHA: Faith. Amma uses it with a special emphasis on alertness coupled with loving care of the work in hand

SURYANAMASKAR: A yogic exercise consisting of salutations to the sun

TAPAS: Literally 'heat'. The practice of spiritual austerities

TULASI: The sacred basil plant

VASANA: Residual impression or habit